Written by
VICKI LOW

Illustrated by
MIKE ROOTH

Assistant
ERIKA WALLACE

Parts of this story are set in the Stone Age. Each chapter ends with a non-fiction page that gives more information about what life might have been like at that time.

OXFORD
UNIVERSITY PRESS

ELIETTE BRUNEL-DESCHAMPS

JEAN-MARIE CHAUVET

CHRISTIAN HILLAIRE

HULE

GAR

BEC

DEOR

NATASHA

REAL PEOPLE IN HISTORY

ELIETTE BRUNEL-DESCHAMPS, JEAN-MARIE CHAUVET AND CHRISTIAN HILLAIRE: Three cave explorers who discovered the Chauvet cave complex.

FICTIONAL CHARACTERS

NATASHA: The 13-year-old niece of Eliette. Natasha has a gift, but is unsure how to deal with it.

HULE: A girl from the Stone Age who lives in the Chauvet caves.

GAR: Hule's friend who feels he has something to prove.

BEC: A tribal elder who notices that Hule has something to share with the rest of the tribe.

DEOR: The leader of the tribe.

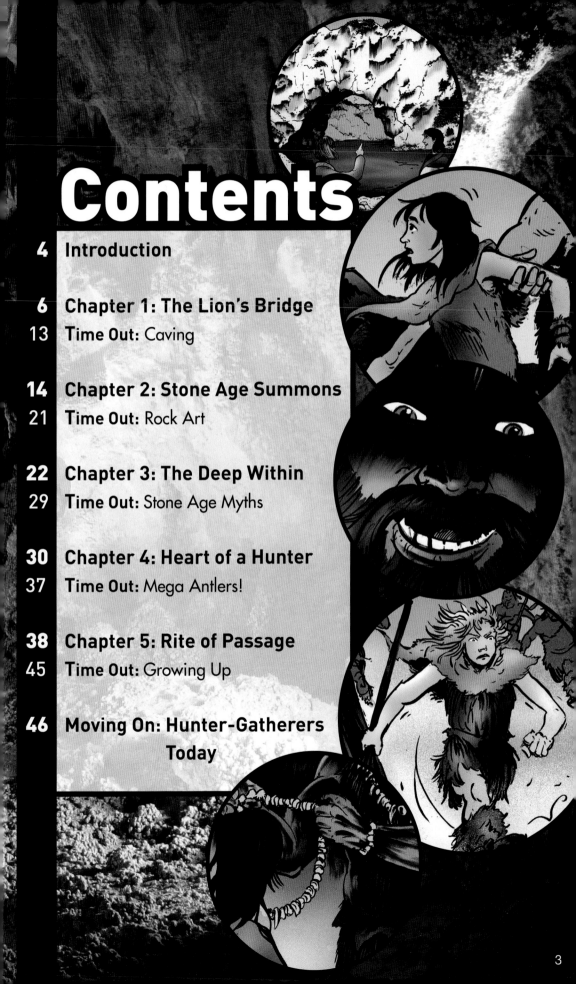

Contents

Thirty thousand years ago, humans lived in small pockets of land across Africa, Europe and Asia. They hunted animals with simple stone tools and gathered plants for food. These humans were the hunter-gatherers of the Stone Age.

Earth was in the middle of the Ice Age. Thick sheets of ice and snow covered the land. Strange animals roamed the icy wastes. Humans found shelter and protection in caves, which they sometimes had to share with other inhabitants.

TIMELINE

The letters BCE stand for 'Before Common Era'. The years before the Common Era are counted backwards, so the greater the number, the longer ago it was. For example, 30,000 BCE is further in the past than 15,000 BCE.

30,000 BC/BCE >>	15,000 BC/BCE >>	13,000 BC/BCE >>	11,000 BC/BCE >>
The Ardèche region of France is inhabited by hunter-gatherers.	Around this time or earlier, cave-dwellers in Lascaux, France, make paintings on rock walls.	Cave paintings in Altamira, Spain, are made by hunter-gatherers.	The Ice Age comes to an end. Many animals become extinct.

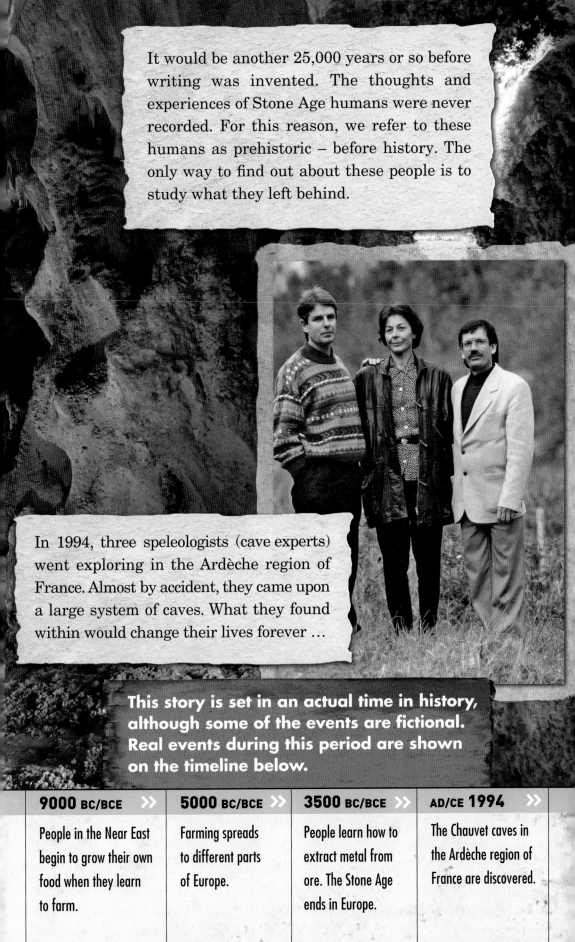

It would be another 25,000 years or so before writing was invented. The thoughts and experiences of Stone Age humans were never recorded. For this reason, we refer to these humans as prehistoric – before history. The only way to find out about these people is to study what they left behind.

In 1994, three speleologists (cave experts) went exploring in the Ardèche region of France. Almost by accident, they came upon a large system of caves. What they found within would change their lives forever ...

This story is set in an actual time in history, although some of the events are fictional. Real events during this period are shown on the timeline below.

9000 BC/BCE »	5000 BC/BCE »	3500 BC/BCE »	AD/CE 1994 »
People in the Near East begin to grow their own food when they learn to farm.	Farming spreads to different parts of Europe.	People learn how to extract metal from ore. The Stone Age ends in Europe.	The Chauvet caves in the Ardèche region of France are discovered.

9

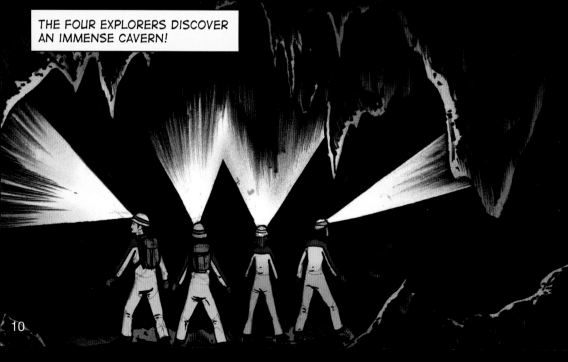

CAVING

There is nothing like the thrill of exploring a cave yourself. You never know what you will find!

Many caves house beautiful rock and mineral formations, rare creatures and sometimes even prehistoric art. Exploring caves builds stamina and strength. For these reasons, caving is a popular sport around the world.

Safety is an important part of caving. Cavers wear protective gear such as helmets, boots and gloves. They always carry spare torches and extra clothing. They work in teams of four. In an accident, one person stays with the injured party while the other two go for help.

WARNING!

Caving has its hazards. Cavers may encounter flooding or unstable rocks. They may get lost or suffer from exhaustion and hypothermia.
Never go caving alone!

13

GAR AND HULE EMERGE FROM THE CAVE. THEY LIVE IN
THE ICE AGE — 30,000 YEARS BEFORE NATASHA'S VISIT.

BEC TAKES HULE DEEP INTO THE CAVES.

THAT'S BECAUSE CHILDREN ARE NOT ALLOWED HERE.

NOW, TELL ME. WHAT OTHER ANIMALS CAN YOU DRAW?

I'VE NEVER BEEN IN THIS PART OF THE CAVE BEFORE.

ALL MY FAVOURITE ANIMALS — BIRDS, HORSES ...

CAN YOU DRAW ME A WOOLLY RHINOCEROS?

HERE, USE THIS. SHOW ME WHAT YOU CAN DO.

OKAY. I LOVE TO DRAW.

HULE DRAWS A WOOLLY RHINOCEROS FOR BEC.

ROCK ART

The paintings in the Chauvet caves were made about 30,000 years ago. But they were far from 'primitive' or crude. They show great artistic skill and a feeling for nature. Some people think these paintings might have been used in rituals. Nobody knows for sure why they were made.

The Chauvet cave-dwellers mostly painted animals. Some were animals they hunted for food, such as mammoths, reindeer and bison. Others were animals they may have feared, such as lions, bears and hyenas.

The Chauvet cave paintings are very important. They help us to understand what life might have been like for our ancestors tens of thousands of years ago. Prehistoric cave paintings have also been found at Lascaux and Cosquer in France, and Altamira in Spain.

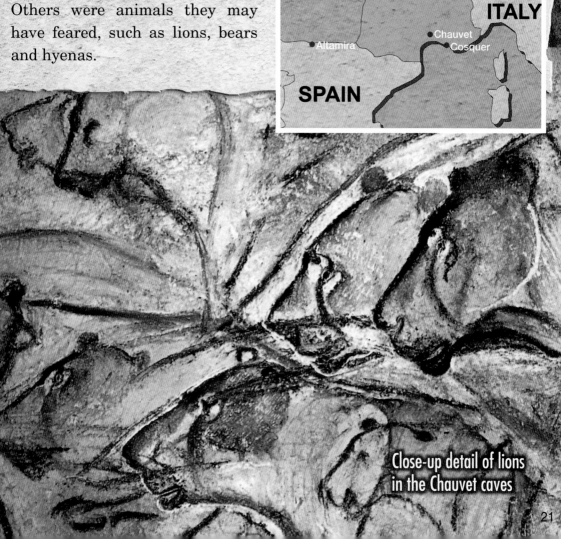

Close-up detail of lions in the Chauvet caves

HULE FOLLOWS THE VOICE — IT IS TOO DARK TO SEE ANYTHING.

COME CLOSER ... CLOSER ...

GASP!

WHO ARE YOU?

MY NAME IS DEOR. YOU'VE NEVER SEEN ME, BUT I AM THE LEADER OF OUR PEOPLE.

ARE YOU A MAN OR AN ANIMAL?

HA, HA, HA! WHILE I AM DRESSED LIKE THIS, I AM BOTH AT ONCE.

I DON'T UNDERSTAND.

SUDDENLY, THEY BOTH HEAR A NOISE.

STONE AGE MYTHS

Do you think of people in the Stone Age as primitive humans who spoke in grunts and whose lives were rough, tough and unhappy? Think again!

MYTH 1: **Stone Age people lived in caves.** They did, but only some of the time. They also made temporary shelters out of branches and animal skins, probably for use in the summer.

MYTH 2: **Stone Age people found it hard to survive.** They knew a great deal about their environments and where to find food even in difficult times. They were nomads who moved with the seasons. They wandered to places where food was most plentiful.

MYTH 3: **Life in the Stone Age was primitive.** Certainly, Stone Age people lacked many things that we have, but their lives were rich and complex. The carvings and paintings they left behind show artistic vision and technical skill. They probably liked to tell elaborate stories and followed many rituals and traditions. They found an effective way to record information – through their drawings.

GAR TAKES A SPEAR FROM THE CAVE.

THIS WILL DO!

I'LL PROVE TO ALL OF YOU THAT I AM A MAN!

GAR ANNOUNCES HIS PLAN TO HUNT A MEGALOCEROS (MEG-AH-LOSS-ER-OSS).

I'M GOING OUT TO HUNT! I'LL FIND A MEGALOCEROS. JUST YOU WAIT AND SEE!

BACK INSIDE THE CAVE, BEC SHOWS HULE HOW TO PREPARE THE CAVE WALL FOR PAINTING.

THE ROCK IS SOFT. YOU CAN SCRAPE AWAY THE BUMPS TO MAKE A SMOOTH SURFACE.

I SEE. IT WILL MAKE DRAWING EASIER.

SOMETIMES, YOU DON'T WANT TO SCRAPE IT AWAY. THIS ROCK WANTS TO HAVE A BEAR DRAWN ON IT. CAN YOU SEE IT?

I SEE WHAT YOU MEAN!

DON'T HURRY. STUDY THE WALL UNTIL YOU KNOW WHAT IT WANTS TO BE.

OKAY ... I'LL TRY.

HULE LOOKS HARD AT THE WALL, THEN CLOSES HER EYES TO THINK.

MEANWHILE, GAR IS OUT LOOKING FOR GAME.

THAT'S MY QUARRY!

PSST, GAR!

FATHER!

WE'RE HERE TO HELP YOU.

BUT I WANT TO DO THIS BY MYSELF ... TO PROVE I CAN!

I KNOW, GAR. BUT HUNTING IS TEAMWORK. NO MAN EVER TOOK A MEGALOCEROS BY HIMSELF.

GO ON, SON. YOU LEAD, WE'LL FOLLOW.

GAR TAKES OFF SWIFTLY AFTER IT. HE IS DETERMINED!

FOR HOURS, THE MEGALOCEROS RUNS — WITH GAR IN STEADY PURSUIT.

BACK IN THE CAVE, HULE CREATES HER FIRST WORK OF ART FOR HER PEOPLE. IT IS THE HARDEST THING SHE HAS EVER DONE.

WITH HUGE, HEAVY ANTLERS ON ITS HEAD, THE MEGALOCEROS CANNOT RUN FOREVER. IT FINALLY SINKS TO ITS KNEES, EXHAUSTED.

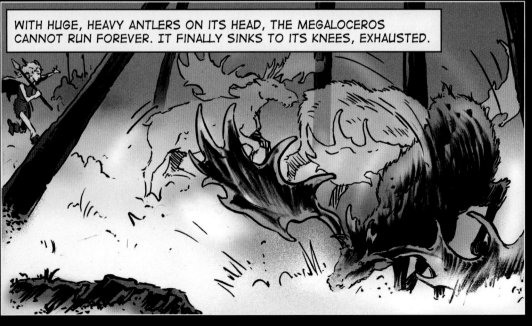

MEGA ANTLERS!

The megaloceros once lived across northern Europe and Asia. It was the largest deer that ever lived, standing 2.13 m at the shoulder. Its antlers measured up to 3.66 m from tip to tip!

Early humans hunted the megaloceros and made paintings of it. Many fossils of this animal have been found in Ireland. For this reason, the megaloceros is also called the Irish elk. It became extinct about 10,500 years ago.

People used to think this giant deer died out because of its huge antlers. They believed the antlers got stuck in trees or were simply so heavy that the megaloceros could not hold up its head!

Scientists now believe the megaloceros died out at the end of the Ice Age. This was a time when the climate changed and food became scarce.

YOU DID IT!

GAR SINKS TO HIS KNEES, EXHAUSTED.

YES, FATHER. BUT I FEEL SORRY FOR THE MEGALOCEROS. HE WANTED TO LIVE, JUST LIKE WE DO.

YOU HAVE THE HEART OF A TRUE HUNTER, GAR.

A TRUE HUNTER FEELS A SPECIAL BOND WITH THE ANIMAL HE HUNTS.

HE IS DEEPLY GRATEFUL FOR THE LIFE HE TAKES.

YOU'RE A MAN NOW, GAR. YOU'VE PROVEN IT.

NIGHT FALLS. THE PEOPLE PERFORM A CEREMONIAL DANCE AROUND THE FIRE.

HULE AND GAR ARE HONOURED GUESTS IN THE CIRCLE!

YOU SEE THIS NECKLACE? IT SYMBOLISES OUR PEOPLE.

MAY THE TIES THAT BIND US NEVER LOOSEN ...

THANK YOU, DEOR.

AND MAY WE NEVER FORGET THE DEBT WE OWE TO MOTHER NATURE.

NEVER, DEOR. THANK YOU.

AND SPRAYS THE RED LIQUID OVER THE HANDS OF GAR AND HULE.

BFFT!

THE CEREMONY IS OVER! GAR AND HULE ARE WELCOMED AS ADULTS INTO THEIR TRIBE.

NATASHA! NATASHA, ARE YOU ALL RIGHT?

WE'VE BEEN SO WORRIED ABOUT YOU! YOU PASSED OUT FOR A FEW MINUTES.

A FEW MINUTES?

IT SEEMED LIKE DAYS.

DAYS? WHAT DO YOU MEAN? TELL US WHAT HAPPENED!

I ... I THINK I'VE HAD A DREAM.

GROWING UP

When does a child become an adult? Is it when you leave school, get a driving licence or reach the age of 21? Many cultures have their own coming-of-age rituals.

The Shan people of Burma and Thailand celebrate Poy Sang Long. For three days, boys are dressed as princes and are carried about on their fathers' shoulders. Then they take religious vows and enter a monastery for a week or more.

An Apache Native American girl becomes a woman in the Sunrise Ceremony. For four days, she sings, dances and runs in ceremonies. She also has cattail pollen – a special plant pollen that is sacred to the Apache – sprinkled on her.

The Pacific islanders of Vanuatu have a ritual called Naghol. Young men dive off a 23-metre high platform with a vine tied to their legs to stop them just short of the ground. After a boy's dive, his mother throws away his favourite toy, showing that he is now an adult.

HUNTER-GATH

Around 11,000 years ago, people began farming and settling in cities. About 5,000 years ago, humans learned how to work metal. The Stone Age came to an end.

The switch from hunting and gathering to farming did not happen everywhere or all at once. In fact, there are still small groups of people around the world today who are hunter-gatherers. Meet these special groups of people:

Kalahari bushmen hunting

The Kalahari Bushmen of southern Africa are able to track animals across all kinds of terrain. They have a rich tradition of storytelling and rock painting.

The Sentinelese live in the Andaman Islands in the Indian Ocean. They avoid any contact with outsiders. After the 2004 tsunami, a helicopter flew low to investigate, but a Sentinelese islander pointed a bow and arrow at the helicopter, as a warning to stay away.

The Huaorani people of the Amazon rainforest hunt with blowpipes. Their arrows are tipped with a poison called curare, which is also used in Western medicine. The Huaorani have many myths about the animals and plants around them.

Hunter-gatherers have a great deal of knowledge about the natural world. They wish to continue the way of life they have followed for thousands of years. It is important that they are allowed to do so.

A Huaorani man teaching survival techniques

INDEX

GLOSSARY

crude – rough, unpolished, unfinished

extinct – a species that has died out and no longer exists

hunter-gatherers – people who live off wild plants and by hunting wild animals, rather than having farms or crops

hypothermia – illness brought on by extreme cold, sometimes it is fatal

immense cavern – a large and dark cave

inhabitants – humans or animals that live in a certain place

mineral formations – rock shapes such as stalactites and stalagmites formed by dripping water in caves

myths – a traditional tale or belief involving fictional people and events

prehistoric – a time before written historical records

primitive – at an early stage of civilisation

rite of passage – an event marking a special stage of a person's life, such as becoming an adult

sacred – something that is holy and respected

speleologists – cave explorers and experts

Stone Age – a period in history when people used stone to make tools

summons – an urgent call to do something